AR PTS: 0.5

D0459119

Fact Finders®

The
Solar System
and Beyond

The Planets
of Our
Solar System

by Steve Kortenkamp

Consultant:
Dr. Ilia I. Roussev
Associate Astronomer
Institute for Astronomy
University of Hawaii at Manoa

CAPSTONE PRESS
a capstone imprint

Fact Finders are published by Capstone Press,
151 Good Counsel Drive, P.O. Box 669, Mankato, Minnesota 56002.
www.capstonepub.com

 Books published by Capstone Press are manufactured with paper
containing at least 10 percent post-consumer waste.

Library of Congress Cataloging-in-Publication Data
Kortenkamp, Steve.
 The planets of our solar system / by Steve Kortenkamp.
  p. cm.—(Fact finders. The solar system and beyond)
 Includes bibliographical references and index.
 Summary: "Describes the eight planets in our solar system, including the birth
of the solar system and the planets' orbits around the Sun"—Provided by publisher.
 ISBN 978-1-4296-5396-1 (library binding)
 ISBN 978-1-4296-6241-3 (paperback)
 1. Planets—Juvenile literature. 2. Solar system—Juvenile literature. I. Title. II. Series.
 QB602.K67 2011
 523.4—dc22   2010026022

Editorial Credits
Jennifer Besel, editor; Heidi Thompson, designer; Laura Manthe, production specialist

Photo Credits
Alamy: B.A.E. Inc., 5; Capstone Press, 11; DigitalVision, 29; ESA, 27; NASA, 12 (inset), 15, 16–17, 19, 23,
24; NASA/Johns Hopkins University/Applied Physics Laboratory/Carnagie Institution of Washington,
13; NASA: JPL, 14 (inset), T. Pyle (SSC), 6–7; NASA/JPL/University of Arizona, cover, 1, 20 (inset),
21, 22 (inset); NASA/JPL-Caltech/Cornell, 17 (inset); NASA/Lawrence Sromovsky, University of
Wisconsin-Madison/ W. M. Keck Observatory, 25; Photo Researchers, Inc: BSIP, 8–9;
Photodisc, 3

Artistic Effects
iStockphoto: appleuzr, Dar Yang Yan, Nickilford

Printed in the United States of America in North Mankato, Minnesota.
062011   006222R

Table of Contents

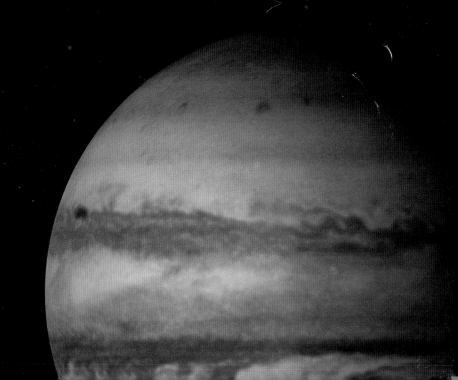

Chapter 1

Wanderers

As night falls, thousands of twinkling lights fill the sky. Those lights are stars in the Milky Way **galaxy**. The stars form patterns in the sky called constellations. Night after night, year after year, most stars stay in the same constellations. But five do not.

If you watch the night sky long enough, you'll notice that five bright stars are different from the others. Over many nights they slowly wander through the constellations. Ancient people called these five stars planets, which to them meant "wandering stars."

Today we know these five are not stars at all. They are the planets Mercury, Venus, Mars, Jupiter, and Saturn. Two more planets, Uranus and Neptune, are too faint to see with your eye. You need a telescope to see them. Together with Earth they are the eight planets in our solar system.

galaxy: a large group of stars and planets

Birth of Our Solar System

About 5 billion years ago there was no Sun, no planets, and no solar system. Instead, in their place in the Milky Way there was a molecular cloud. This cloud slowly began to collapse, like a balloon shrinking as it loses air. Most of the gas and dust in the shrinking cloud collected in the center and got very hot. When the gas in the center reached 18 million degrees Fahrenheit (10 million degrees Celsius), it started to burn. Our Sun was born!

The rest of the gas and dust in the cloud fell into a flat disk swirling around the Sun. Dust began to stick together to make rocks. Then rocks bumped together and clumped into bigger boulders. Soon round objects emerged from the swarm of colliding boulders. Small planets were born! Four small, rocky planets were made from the dust contained in the Sun's inner disk.

molecular cloud: a giant cloud made mostly of hydrogen atoms bound together

Farther out from the Sun, the disk was a lot bigger and colder. There was more dust. Some of the gas froze into ice and mixed with the dust. Out of the dust and ice grew four more planets. The planets were bigger than the four of the inner disk. These bigger planets had stronger **gravity**. They pulled in hydrogen and helium gases from the disk.

gravity: a force that pulls objects together

Moving Together

Our Sun is a star at the center of our solar system. Eight planets travel through space on **orbits** that circle the Sun. Mercury is the closest planet to the Sun. Venus, Earth, and Mars are the next three planets out. These four rocky planets are the inner planets. Next come the four outer planets—Jupiter, Saturn, Uranus, and Neptune.

orbit: the path an object follows as it goes around the Sun

Mercury

Venus

Earth

Mars

Jupite

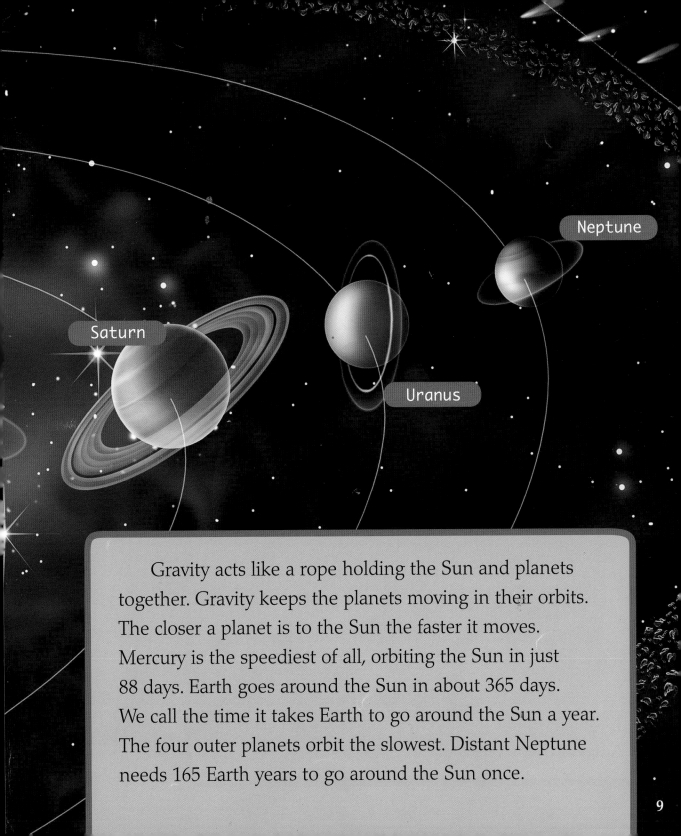

Saturn

Uranus

Neptune

Gravity acts like a rope holding the Sun and planets together. Gravity keeps the planets moving in their orbits. The closer a planet is to the Sun the faster it moves. Mercury is the speediest of all, orbiting the Sun in just 88 days. Earth goes around the Sun in about 365 days. We call the time it takes Earth to go around the Sun a year. The four outer planets orbit the slowest. Distant Neptune needs 165 Earth years to go around the Sun once.

Planets rotate like spinning tops. Look at the sky. Can you tell Earth is rotating? When you watch a sunrise, you are not seeing the Sun move. Instead, you are standing on Earth, and Earth is spinning you around. When you're on the side of Earth that is facing the Sun, it's daytime. When you're on the side that's facing away, it's night. In 24 hours, Earth rotates completely around one time. That's one day.

Every planet has daytime and nighttime. But each planet spins at a different speed. Jupiter has the shortest day. It spins around in less than 10 hours. Other planets have much longer days. A day on Venus lasts about 2,800 hours.

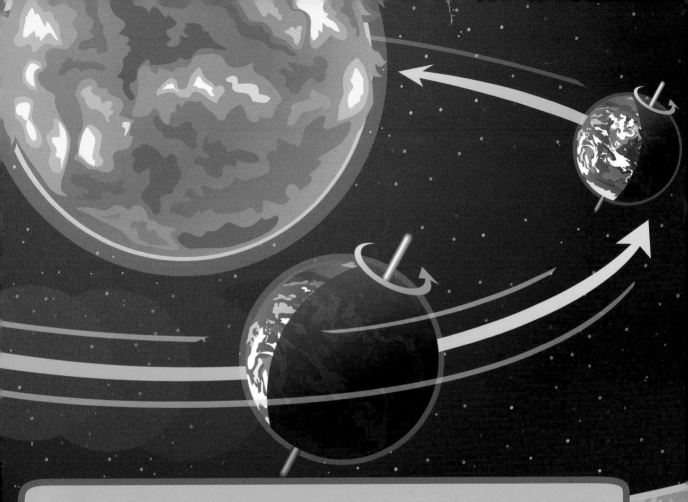

Planet	Length of Day (sunrise to sunrise)	Length of Year (once around the Sun)
Mercury	4,224 hours	88 Earth days
Venus	2,800 hours	224 Earth days
Earth	24 hours	365 Earth days
Mars	24 hours, 30 minutes	687 Earth days
Jupiter	9 hours, 55 minutes	4,330 Earth days
Saturn	10 hours, 39 minutes	10,755 Earth days
Uranus	18 hours	30,685 Earth days
Neptune	16 hours	60,190 Earth days

Chapter 2

The Inner Planets

Astronomers use what they know about Earth to help them understand other planets. They look for features other planets might have in common with Earth. They look for **atmospheres**, rocky surfaces, or iron **cores**. By studying these features we know that three planets in our solar system are very much like Earth. These are the three other inner planets—Mercury, Venus, and Mars.

Mercury

Like Earth, Mercury has an iron core surrounded by a rocky surface. Round craters cover the planet's surface. The craters formed when asteroids and comets hit Mercury. Space probes show that Mercury also has volcanoes, mountains, and high cliffs.

an up-close view of Mercury's craters

atmosphere: the gases that surround a planet or star

core: the inner part of a planet

Unlike Earth, Mercury does not have an atmosphere. Earth's atmosphere acts like a blanket, keeping heat in at night. Without this blanket of gas, Mercury gets very cold at night. Temperatures on the side facing away from the Sun drop to -275°F (-171°C). But Mercury is the closest planet to the Sun. During the daytime, temperatures soar to more than 800°F (427°C)!

Venus

Venus is a rocky planet almost the same size as Earth. It is often called Earth's twin planet. Venus is also Earthlike because it has volcanoes and mountains. And it has an atmosphere with clouds and lightning.

But there are a few things that make Venus very different from Earth. Compared to Earth, Venus rotates backward. That means the Sun rises in the west on Venus, not in the east like on Earth. On Venus the clouds are made of **acid** while Earth's clouds are made of water. The atmosphere on Venus is almost 100 times thicker than Earth's. This thick atmosphere traps so much heat that the surface of Venus is about 850°F (454°C). Venus is so hot that any oceans it once had have all boiled away. Venus is now totally dry.

a lava flow from Venus' volcanoes

acid: a substance that can burn your skin

The *Venera 7* was a spacecraft from the former Soviet Union. It landed on Venus in 1970. It was the first spacecraft to ever land on another planet.

Mars

Mars is the planet in our solar system most like Earth. Its rocky surface has deep canyons, tall mountains, and huge volcanoes. In fact, the largest volcano in the solar system is on Mars. Mars also has a thin atmosphere with clouds made of water. Snow sometimes falls from the clouds. At the North and South poles, snow and ice form thick polar caps, just like the polar caps on Earth.

Earth and Mars both go through long cold and warm cycles. Millions of years ago, Mars was a warm, wet planet, like Earth is today. Space probes sent to Mars have sent back pictures of dried-up riverbeds, lakes, and shorelines. But there is very little water on the planet today. Mars is in a cold part of the cycle. Nearly all its water is frozen underground and in the polar ice caps. The whole planet is a cold, dry, dusty desert.

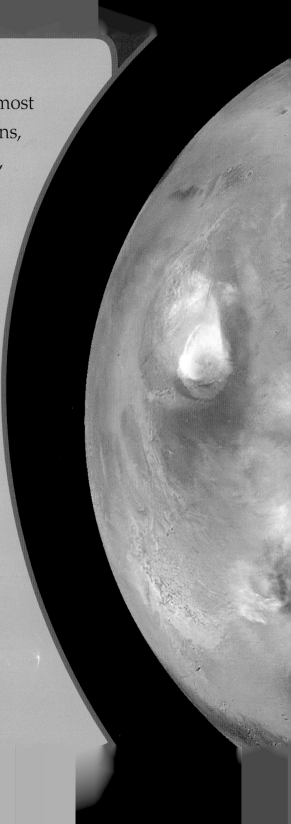

FACT: Winds on Mars sometimes make giant dust storms that cover the entire planet.

a close-up view of Mars' surface

Chapter 3

The Outer Planets

The four planets farthest from the Sun are very different from Earth. These giant planets are much bigger than the inner planets. Giant planets have extremely strong gravity. This force pulls huge amounts of gas into a round shape. That means giant planets don't have rocky, solid surfaces. The outer layers of giant planets are made mostly of gases such as hydrogen and helium. That's why some people call them gas giants.

Scientists send space probes to study the outer planets. The probes use parachutes to fall slowly through the gas layers of a giant planet. Inside the planets, the gases get thicker and hotter. The gases eventually turn into a soupy mixture as thick as syrup. Probes that go into giant planets don't come out. They are crushed and melted by the pressure and heat of the thick gas.

Neptune

Uranus

Jupiter

Saturn

Jupiter

Jupiter is the biggest planet in our solar system. It is so big that more than 1,000 Earths could fit inside it! One probe parachuting into Jupiter sent back information about the clouds and lightning storms. The probe measured winds of 450 miles (724 km) per hour in the clouds of Jupiter. That's twice as fast as the strongest winds ever measured on Earth!

Jupiter's gravity holds more than 60 moons in orbit around the planet. One moon named Io (EYE-oh) is covered with volcanoes. Some molten lava erupts off Io and goes into space around Jupiter. Particles from the lava fall onto the North and South poles of Jupiter. When the particles hit Jupiter's atmosphere, they light up in colorful streams in the planet's sky.

Jupiter's moon Io

A single storm in Jupiter's atmosphere, called the Great Red Spot, is larger than the entire Earth.

Great Red Spot

Saturn

Saturn stands apart from the other giant planets because of its rings. All four giant planets have rings, but Saturn's are the biggest and brightest. From Earth it looks like Saturn has one or two large rings. But space probes showed Saturn has millions of them. The rings contain billions of ice pieces. Saturn's rings formed when a small object, such as a moon or comet, got too close to the planet. Saturn's strong gravity shattered the object into tiny pieces. Those pieces now orbit the planet.

Like Jupiter, Saturn also has more than 60 moons. The biggest is Titan. Even though Titan is a moon, two things make it an Earthlike world. First, it has an atmosphere a lot like Earth's was in its early history. Titan has clouds, storms, and rain. Second, Titan is the only other place in our solar system where astronomers have found lakes and seas. But Titan's lakes don't hold water. Storms on Titan rain liquid methane that fills the lakes.

Saturn's moon Titan

FACT: On Earth methane is a gas burned for heating and cooking. Titan is so cold that methane turns to liquid and falls from the clouds as rain.

Uranus and Neptune

Uranus and Neptune are the smallest of the giant planets. Each of them is only about four times bigger than Earth. They are also the farthest planets from the Sun. That makes them the coldest planets. Neptune also has the strongest winds in the solar system. The planet's winds reach speeds of 1,240 miles (2,000 km) per hour.

Neptune

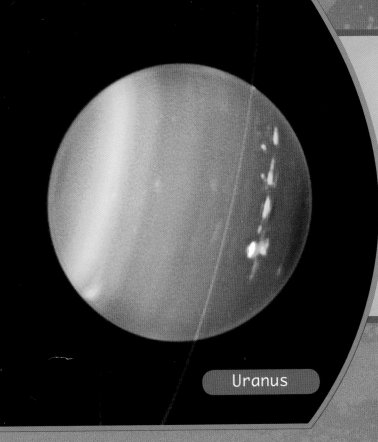

Uranus

Uranus is the most tilted planet. It spins completely tipped over on its side. No one knows how this happened. Long ago Uranus may have been hit by another planet that knocked it over.

Comparing the Planets

Planet	Temperature	Moons	Rings
Mercury	low: -297°F (-183°C) high: 801°F (427°C)	0	0
Venus	864°F (462°C)	0	0
Earth	low: -126°F (-88°C) high: 136°F (58°C)	1	0
Mars	low: -125°F (-87°C) high: 23°F (-5°C)	2	0
Jupiter	-234°F (-148°C)	more than 60	4
Saturn	-288°F (-178°C)	more than 60	millions
Uranus	-357°F (-216°C)	27	11
Neptune	-353°F (-214°C)	13	4

Chapter 4

Discoveries

Are there other planets orbiting our Sun? Some scientists think so. Thousands of tiny, cold, dark planets could be orbiting near the edge of our system.

Scientists do know there are other planets in the Milky Way galaxy. Astronomers have already discovered more than 400 planets orbiting stars near our Sun. These extrasolar planets are beyond our solar system.

Almost all the extrasolar planets are as big as the giant planets in our solar system. These planets are strange worlds very different from our own planets. Many orbit very close to their stars. Being so close to their stars makes most extrasolar planets really hot. The hottest are more than 4,000°F (2,200°C). Scientists call these scorching extrasolar giant planets hot-Jupiters.

super-Earth
Gliese 581g

Astronomers have also found some smaller extrasolar planets they call super-Earths. Super-Earths are rocky planets that are bigger than Earth. A star named Gliese (GLEE-zuh) 581 has six super-Earths orbiting it, much like the four Earthlike planets orbiting our Sun. No one knows yet if these super-Earths have oceans, continents, or life.

Amazing Planets

Scientists have learned so much about the planets since ancient people noticed those five wandering stars. Space probes have given us close-up looks at the surfaces of the inner planets. Other probes have explored the giant outer planets. Maybe probes will one day find hidden planets in our solar system.

With so many stars in the Milky Way galaxy, maybe scientists will find a planet like Earth. A planet that's not too hot or too cold. A planet with deep oceans of water and an atmosphere with oxygen. Maybe there will be living creatures on that planet looking back—wondering about the planets going around our Sun.

Glossary

acid (AS-id)—a substance that tastes sour and can burn your skin

asteroid (AS-tuh-royd)—a large space rock that moves around the Sun; most asteroids are not round enough to be called planets

atmosphere (AT-muh-sfeer)—the layer of gases that surrounds some dwarf planets, moons, planets, and stars

core (KOR)—the inner part of a dwarf planet, planet, or star

galaxy (GAL-uhk-see)—a large group of stars and planets

gravity (GRAV-uh-tee)—a force that pulls objects together; gravity increases as the mass of objects increases or as objects get closer

molecular cloud (muh-LEK-yuh-lur KLOUD)—a cloud trillions of miles across made mostly of hydrogen atoms bound together; new stars form deep within the cores of molecular clouds

orbit (OR-bit)—the path an object follows as it goes around a dwarf planet, planet, or star

probe (PROHB)—a small vehicle used to explore objects in outer space

Read More

Carson, Mary Kay. *Extreme Planets! Q&A*. New York: HarperCollins, 2008.

Kortenkamp, Steve. *The Dwarf Planets*. The Solar System and Beyond. Mankato, Minn.: Capstone Press, 2011.

Oxlade, Chris. *Space Watch: Planets*. Eye on Space. New York: PowerKids Press, 2010.

Tourville, Amanda Doering. *Exploring the Solar System*. Let's Explore Science. Vero Beach, Fla.: Rourke Pub., 2011.

Internet Sites

FactHound offers a safe, fun way to find Internet sites related to this book. All of the sites on FactHound have been researched by our staff.

Here's all you do:

Visit *www.facthound.com*

Type in this code: 9781429653961

Check out projects, games and lots more at
www.capstonekids.com

Index